GET BENT

Published by BG Press
ISBN 978-1-945028-48-9

Editors: Robert Vaughan (Editor-in-Chief), and Meg Tuite (Fiction Editor)
Cover paintings by Robert Vaughan
Book design by Adam Robinson for goodbookdevelopers.com

Contents

GET BENT

a new anthology
from Bending Genres

edited by **Robert Vaughan** and Meg Tuite

Robert Vaughan
FOREWORD

In 1979, the play, *BENT*, premiered in London at the Royal Court Theatre. That same year, it transferred to Broadway. I attended a liberal State University in upstate New York, and in the early 1980s, we took on this controversial and cutting-edge play. I was cast as Wolf (Wolfgang Granz), a handsome member of the upper echelon of the Sturmabteilung corps. One evening, the lead player, Max, much to the resentment of his partner, Rudy, brings home Wolf from the Berlin bars. Simultaneously, that same night, Hitler orders the assassination of the upper members of the Sturmabteilung corps.

The following morning, there are rapid-fire knocks on the door. The men stumble out of the bedroom as the SS men knock down their front door. My character, Wolf, is shot several times, and falls dramatically over the sofa to his death.

This experience altered my life in several ways. It was the first and last time I played a character who dies onstage. It was also at the early onset of the AIDS Epidemic, which was first acknowledged in the *New York Times* in 1982. The title of the play, *Bent*, is a slang word used in some European countries to refer to homosexuals. At the time the play was first performed, there was very little historical research or even awareness about the Nazi persecution of homosexuals. In many ways, Martin Sherman's play, *Bent*, helped to increase the education and expand that research in the 1980s and 1990s.

Thus, in some roundabout way, we come to our new Bending Genres anthology, *Get Bent*. We hope you enjoy the diverse, odd, inventive assortment of genre-bending work included within these pages. And much like the play, *Bent*, shifted my perspective, may this tome be the same for you.

Dominique Christina
PERIOD POEM: PART 2

Be not deceived.
We ARE witches.
That, is no hallucination.
Don't let the pink hats fool you
We get busy
I, Tituba
West Indian slave woman
Born this time with bigger hands,
Haunting the men who've loved me,
They will never stop saying my name.

We, loose women
Crawl out of graves
Every morning—
That's feminism

The cemeteries in Salem
Are all empty—
That's resurrection.

The slight of hand magic
The charred bone bayonet
Waiting beneath the earth...

We DO ride the wind,
Conjure and tilt the world,
Croon a midnight curse,
Sizzle a blood ritual,
Curate a menstrual anthem,
Pull peonies from between our thighs
Middle finger in the air matriarchal madness
We get busy

What matters is how we don't die
What matters is how many of us died
What matters is Eve's sworn statement—
The apocryphal testimony of
A borrowed rib
The sweet meat symphony of forbidden fruit

When a woman defies God,
That's genetics.

Everything after, is blood.

The greedy chattering
Of cervix and uterus
Of shedding and reinventing
Of cramping and oozing
Of maxi pad and diva cup

I bled
On a sky blue jumpsuit
On a busy street corner in Jersey
On purpose—
That was conjure

I spouted like a geyser on a stage
In Philly and never stopped reading
My poem-
That WAS my poem
My sex
My womanhood
My genius body
That's how I woman as a witch.
You gon have to confront my blood.

I took an oath
From my mama's
Excalibur womb
Inherited a war between my legs
There will always be stains on the sheets.

So let the good girls who cross
Their legs in church howl a red stitched amen
Let the women teetering on the edge
Of menopause tabernacle their
Wet labia to star shine

Blessed be the blood and
How it runneth over
Blessed be the slipknot crimson chaos
Blessed be the Red Sea riddle
The dragons we ride
The scales and clots
That know when to leave

Blessed be the body
The cult magic of woman
The pomegranate molasses
The scarlet chariot
The needling harp

Blessed be the 28th day.
Blessed be the full moon sonnet of woman
Blessed be the beleaguered body
The lexicon of survivors
The un-crucified

There is no shame in
Letting the body be the body
No shame in
Honeying the hive between our legs
I Jezebel the blood
I Medusa ANY man
Who says we should bleed in secret
I Magdalene the god box under my skirt
I let the nectar decorate my thighs
I holy
I unholy
I sacrilege
I curse the curse

I roll the stone away
I night sky broom stick ride and ride
I make my blood my belonging
I witchcraft bleed and bleed

My Sisyphean uterus repeats itself
Every month I say, amen.
Sacred tongue, give me
A better word for sorcery
That, is the story of my blood.
Sacred heart, give me
A better word for woman
That, is the story of the world.

Be not deceived.
We ARE witches.
That is no hallucination.
Resurrection is always insurrection.
We are no longer afraid
To bleed…

Ryan Griffith
BLOODSONGS

American Anger

For dinner they served burning midnight, cavesongs. The general stoked our tumors. We touched stillborns, strangled dresses. We sang lullabies to x-rays. The coroner's daughter showed us the wired dark, gold mines, nightingales.

The Coroner's Daughter

Her birthmarks are victorian brides. Glass pastures in her eyes, blue as french cigarettes, coronations. The bell ringer's son is at the door, priests in the bearded dark. Memory is the most elegant crucifixion.

French Cigarettes

Strike a match off a cat's eye. The orderlies are smoking novocaine, blood clots.

Novocaine

The arsonists and their butane tenderness. Mother of dawn with her tongue cut out, we seek malachite, verdigris, buckthorn. Glyphs of skin.

Verdigris

The Jerusalem of a throat. Those storms in your sockets, birdshit, beeswax, and kidney fat. Mechanized leviathan. Time tears through our green religion.

Jerusalem

Tourniquet lover, only you will survive these scribes of fire. We are handcuffed to the night.

Scribe

You are the last sick story written in my cells.

Sara Lippmann

PARACHUTES

When I turn six, my mother starts school. She walks me to my classroom for the first and last time. After today, I'm on my own. A stringer for the local paper snaps our photo. We wear backpacks like parachutes. The caption reads: *like mother, like daughter.*

Fish slosh in the toilet. Fish we flushed, an unlucky pair born in Ziploc, blanched at the glimpse of holiday Gefilte, as if to say: *how could you?* My grandparents read German fairytales. There are worse things. Children on fire. Don't play with matches, they say. Children starve to death protesting dinner peas, but this fish, this floppy gold fellow, is Jonah in scale. Back from the dead. Shut the lid, they say. Walk away before it comes for you.

My mother says, Pay Attention. She is studying how to help kids with problems. I am her guinea pig. Not because I have problems, mind you, but because I'm a kid. Later, she will bring me into dream analysis class for show & tell. Remember. Recall. Draw what you know.

Cliffs, teeth, bloody gums. Tarantulas and snakes. House on Fire. In dreams I am falling, being chased. Textbook dreams. My dreams are disappointing, lacking in case worthy Complexity. In dreams my parents wear masks, funny rubber, Their cheeks burning coals like Ronald and Nancy Reagan on MTV. This is the Land of Confusion. Capes soar. Putty peels from the forehead down. Their faces open onto other faces.

When I stand sweaty, hot over her pillow, my mother pops up. I thought you were a ghost. Go back to sleep. Think happy thoughts. Here's a paper, take a crayon.

Plates crash. My father pulls in and out of the driveway. When you work your fucking balls off it is reasonable to expect dinner on the table. He returns, contrite, with Ding Dongs and frozen entrees. Anger gives way to prayer. His room abuts my room. Walls are thin. At night, I listen to him read from the Torah—Genesis, Numbers—his voice lulling yet nasal, as if his pathway has been blocked.

Jack Tripper makes me happy. *Three's Company* makes me happy. Television is my babysitter. I laugh with my mouth open and blackened in crumbs. My mother is right: with a little practice, you can train your brain to dream anything. Pratfalls and short shorts and baby doll fringes and swinging kitchen doors.

Years from now, I will ask: If you are so unhappy why do you stay? She will say it's complicated and you don't know the half of it, and I will close my eyes and conjure her pushed, banister split, tumbling backwards, downstairs.

The Ku Klux Klan shows up after school. They knock like Jehovah's Witnesses knocks only louder, more forceful. I am a Latchkey kid. *We know you're in there.* The signpost on my door gives away my faith but they won't find me. In the living room, MTV blares. Fists pound but I am deep inside my mother's closet, crouched between dry cleaner bags. When I sketch myself hidden behind a curtain of dresses, suffocating in plastic, long forgotten, my mother gets an A+. Finally, she has material to work with.

You don't need school to know everything signifies something else. Vanity. Fear. There are categories. It is false to go around puffing stuff up with extraneous meaning. Still, people see what they want.

I am in a barrel floating downstream. I am in Ireland in winter, in Ibiza in summer, on a scooter, a wicker between the handlebars, hibiscus in my hair. I pedal fast and faster, as if the wheels might miraculously grant me lift.

When swastikas crop up on the playground equipment near my daughter's school, I say, don't worry. Things happen. You are safe. My daughter goes to a school named after a female paratrooper in World War II. Before Hannah Senesh was killed by the Nazis, she was tortured for enemy secrets. She never told. Instead she wrote poetry. This line's hers: *A voice called and I went.*

I am failing Shakespeare in college. I can't get to class because I'm nursing. I am always nursing and when I'm not nursing I'm being puked on. There is no time. I live in a dorm but forget my dorm key. I can't get a new key because duh, I'm a mother now. I've had my chance.

The vivid dreamscape is a side effect of my new antidepressant. I'm told. Don't you understand: Everything is a trade-off.

My husband is cheating with my best friend. She is in real estate so we are drinking wine in a mid-century modern overlooking the valley, somehow in California. They lay out the new world order. Marriage should be a lease, not a purchase. My merlot drops from my hand. The difference between glass and crystal lies in the drama of its shatter.

Before bed, my daughter reads to me and to her stuffed animals, among them, the tattered bear I had as a child. This is my gift to her. Proximity is enough. That smell. She does all the voices. I'm out like a light.

Last night, the land of dreams is at once unknown and familiar. Leafy ferns and ficus, lush and green like Rousseau only minus the beasts. Rousseau never left his house anyway. The only animals here are women: on the bed, on the floor, arms flung overhead in reckless abandon. I tiptoe. I do not wish to disturb. There is a blue basket of mushrooms on the countertop. Ingredients for dinner. I pop the stems and launch the caps out the window. They catch wind and drift. The sky is full of them.

previously pub. at *Diagram*

Wendy Oleson
WORDS YOU TAUGHT ME

Rubes: People who disgusted you.

Gorge: What rose when people disgusted you.

Y-M-C-Ack: The place where the rubes prattled on—especially in the women's locker room—and made your gorge rise. You were a magnet for spit-talkers. The sight of blood running down a leg.

The Y-IRE: The monthly newsletter published by our YMCA—you taught me to be enraged by the name of it.

Philistines: People who didn't agree "The Y-IRE" should be renamed "The Y Wire" or "The Yer." Also, what you called our friends who hadn't read Ray Bradbury.

Christ figure: A central character in most art—especially prestige TV—which you said employed a significant Judeo-Christian undergirding. In your mind, there would always be a Christ figure and a devil. You referred to a work colleague as Beelzebub. But you also started me on the Hainish Cycle by Ursula K. Le Guin, who studied Taoism.

Flinky: A snack cracker, pretzel, or chip. You said "salty flinky" to mock the kind of sci-fi you did not like because it used too many made-up words. Occasionally, you felt this applied to Ursula K. Le Guin.

Bougainvillea: What was running up the staircase of the apartment building, the one where we shared a wall. Originally from the Midwest, I'd never seen it. The veined leaves reminded me of the skin—purple, magenta, ruby—of another world. It's of the "four o'clock family," which means it opens in the late afternoon and closes by morning.

Friendship: A word with very little stability, like freedom and fun, love and pain. Is it friendship if we haven't spoken in years?

Vouchsafing: The way I granted you all that misplaced admiration.

Gaslight: What the blonde woman was doing to you with those voicemail messages you played for me; what all your exes had done. You were very good to the people who hurt you, and I hated that.

Wraiths: The souls of the dead we never saw. Still, some of our neighbors claimed the building was haunted. Some nights I heard tapping on the wall we shared, but that was you saying goodnight. I knocked back, a silly rhythm. What a comfort to know you were there. Now, I'm not sure where you are, and I don't know the word for what we used to be.

previously pub. at *Maine Review*

Pat Foran

EN AEROPUERTOS

1. Aeropuerto Internacional de la Ciudad de México

I'm in a line, a line of lines, waiting to check in for my flight to Monterrey.

The line isn't moving.

I'm watching a man maneuver a floor machine in and around the line, around all the lines. He's waxing things. The floors, the *federales*, the kiosks, the cat carriers, the jetways, all the ways. He's waxing everything in the airport.

It's freakin' gleaming in here, says the man in line in front of me, panning for gold with his phone. *I'm putting this on Facebook Live.*

Travelers teeter as the line appears to move, but doesn't. The line is wending its way like a waterfall that rises and falls, and falls and rises, before reaching the beginning of the next end.

The woman in line next to me balances a postcard on her left arm and announces what she's about to write: *"Dear Fred... Wish you were here to see this. Then maybe you'd believe it. Maybe you'd believe me."*

The line isn't moving. Like time isn't. Like we aren't.

I think about you and I think about me and I think about us.

We're in a five-panel cartoon. Panel 1: A woman says to a man, *I'm leaving you, do you hear? Leaving.* Panels 2 and 3: The man is there, alone. Panel 4: The man is shown, leaving. Panel 5: The man is gone and the woman is there. *How could you leave me?* she says.

While I think about the woman's cartoonish question—the word *How* hovering above this long, long line in a show of metaphysical force—the sun peeks through the paneled glass and shines on the waxing man in motion, leaving a shadow of fool's gold in the late-afternoon light.

2. Aeropuerto Internacional de Monterrey

I'm at the bar in Wings Aeropuerto Monterrey Terminal A.

What can I do you for? the bartender says.

Tecate Light? I say.

The ear-budded woman seated next to me is talking, maybe to me.

"I am listening to the Voice of America, and I am hearing that tears are like gold," she says, uncertainly. "It's coming out of this small speaker, the Voice is, and it's precious as punch—like a punch-drunk nobleman from a black-and-white world."

The bartender looks at the woman and says, maybe to her, but I think to me: *That Voice of America is thrown. They're throwing it, you know.*

I don't hear a voice, not in this shuddering distance, but I do hear the treasures of the Sierra Madre, a jingle-jangle in the gilded hurt of all the hearts.

The air in this city is thin, so thin. Thin and distant and thrown. Tears evaporate so quickly here. I wonder: Is my nose bleeding?

I also wonder: What is a kiss? Am I alone? Will anyone ever find me?

Buy me a drink? Voice of America Woman asks.

The bartender, whose lips aren't moving, doesn't wait for me to answer.

3. Aeropuerto Internacional de Mérida

I'm on the jetway.

A smiling boy wearing a Poco Loco t-shirt asks me if I am a spy.

No, I am not a spy, I say. *Maybe it's the suit and tie?*

No, the boy says. *It's the way the light in here makes you a shadow and not a man, a shadow and not anything. Except a spy.*

I look at the boy, who continues to smile, and I think about my son, who did not smile often, but when he did, it was gold.

I think about my son and I think about gold and I think about shadows and I think about the sound that is nothing.

I hear it sometimes, this nothing. It echoes in the foothill shrines to *Madre María*. It rings in the weather-beaten prayers for the pristine. It shoots the curl in the clandestine song of the certain. The song of the sure.

The smiling boy laughs and begins to sing. It's an impossible song, imperceptible in the jangle of the jetway.

How come you don't know this one? he asks.

previously pub. at ***Flash Fiction Review***

Tara Stillions Whitehead
ONE MORE INCH OF SHADOW

Joe's uncle bought rain barrels and fertilizer. A.J.'s dad emptied the family checking account, $300 at a time, from the Circle K where he bought cartons of cigarettes, where my brother was robbed at gunpoint on Christmas Eve. My stepmom bought a safe and stocked it with Symphony bars, Energizer batteries, and two-way radios.

Before the New Year's Eve party in Crystal's dad's backyard, Anita helped blow up a kiddie pool and fill it with Epsom salt in case the hospitals got too full and her sister, three days past her due date, would have to give birth at home.

Crystal's dad's beach house was where we decided to avail ourselves of all remaining innocence before the end. We already kept so many secrets there.

"If planes and satellites are going to fall out of the sky," Crystal said, entertaining just for a moment the silly notion that a computer glitch would steal her fate. "I refuse to die a fucking virgin."

Thirty minutes before midnight, I declined a call from my mom at the Vista jail and let Crystal's dad pour the remainder of a handle of Cuervo into my plastic cup. "To be so goddamn young again," he whispered, not to me, but to the sea.

We would learn a lot about the world that didn't end. Like how Crystal's hymen wouldn't break, couldn't break, not without twilight anesthesia. Or how alcohol made Jimmy have seizures and AC/DC gave Janae orgasms. We would learn how Rob took his dad's rifle down to Tamarack Beach, alone, fully loaded. That existential dread was just one more inch of shadow. The cameras at the vet where I bagged dead animals and sterilized scalpels were just dummies—they never caught me slipping vials of ketamine into my scrub pants. They never caught me crying over my mother's voicemails.

Midnight came and went.

Earl shotgunned a beer.

Kelsey swallowed a pill.

Kemp sucked down a can of air duster and plowed his Mitsubishi through the lowered arm of Pendleton's D Gate.

Crystal's dad handed me a cigarette. And then reached for the moon.

"Time is a shrinking knot," he said, crying. "We have to cut our own ends."

The sun stretched its neck as it rose over the silent cul de sac. It reached into the sidewalk cracks and swept through the tired palms.

I stood at the threshold of driveway and asphalt, dumbfounded. I didn't know where to begin again.

It wouldn't take us long to learn that the world doesn't care about prophecies or numbers or our endless methods of self-destruction. The world— thank God—is incapable of making any promise we expect it to keep.

previously pub. in *They More Than Burned*

Leigh Chadwick
I GROW TOMATOES

I like to grow tomatoes, so I go into the backyard & plant a bottle of ketchup. That night I dream I grow gills & wade into the Atlantic & then I am swimming & swimming & swimming until I come across an octopus. I ask the octopus, *If you lost one of your hearts, would you be happier?* The octopus doesn't answer because it's an octopus. When I wake up, I check on the ketchup bottle I planted in the backyard. I run my hand over the soil. I'm getting old enough to think about youth. I think, *Oh, how life dissipates.* I think about high school, I don't remember it, though I remember getting fucked while high in the parking lot of a school. Sometimes something counts. I hate that I know how to spell *tachycardia*. I hate that I know how to spell *malignant* & *hospice* & *goodbye.* I never go to war because I don't think I'd make it home from war. Every Tuesday I miss my mother's mother. Have you ever cried in Pig Latin? Left home for another home? I am 7,224 Twitter followers away from getting a free ride to heaven. When I get there, I will plant an entire field of ketchup bottles. I will forget how to spell everything, even my name.

previously pub. at **Trampset**

Nicholas Claro
OPTICS

Kristen and I still had mutual friends, which is how I heard her uncle died in the first place. After the news, I broke protocol and sent her a message. Our divorce had been finalized over a year ago, and ever since, our interactions have been inconsistent, consisting mostly of politely ignoring one another, like the time I bumped into her in line at the Dillons on 21st and Amidon when I was hungover, buying Pedialyte. She casually pulled an issue of *Us Weekly* from a nearby rack, turned the pages slowly, like she cared about celebrity drama.

I figured like on Instagram and Twitter, she'd blocked me. So the message didn't matter. It was for optics anyway. A way to prove to our mutual friends that I could set aside our past and extend an olive branch during her tough time.

That's all I'd expected from this, something to make me look like a decent human being.

Then Kristen messaged me back: *I haven't been to that restaurant in ages.*

An old pet peeve of mine was how Kristen was always late. I made the reservation for 6:45, and told her it was for 7:00. At 7:17 I'd just finished my second negroni when she walked in. It took me a second to recognize her. Her hair was short. Shortest I'd seen it.

I was nervous. Not quite butterfly nervous, thanks to the drinks.

I stood as she approached the table. My limbs deflated.

"This new carpeting?" she said. "It's so ugly."

I wasn't sure. I appreciated the icebreaker.

"Do we hug?" I said. "Shake hands? High five?"

"We can hug," she said.

Things didn't feel natural at first. Halfway through our first bottle of wine the nervousness waned, and things started to. We jumped through hoops of small talk over fried calamari with a few pauses between sentences. These were brief. The only sounds filling them, the faint, tinkling strikes of silverware against our plates.

Not much later, our entrées arrived along with a second bottle of red. After our waiter refilled our glasses and walked off, I said, "I was sorry to hear about Dean. He was a good guy."

"I have conflicting feelings about the whole thing," she said. "Part grief, part relief that he isn't suffering anymore. Is it normal to feel this way? Does that make me cruel?"

I almost reached across the table to touch her hand.

"No. Not cruel. Not at all." At the risk of making things all about me, a common theme of many old arguments, I added, "I recently experienced the same feeling. A friend of mine succumbed to liver cirrhosis last month."

Kristen swirled the wine around in her glass, nodded.

She cleared her throat. "Anyway," she said. "Enough of all that. What's new with you, Ben?"

I was happy for the change of subject. I just wished my life was more interesting. That I could've carried the conversation. Places I'd visited. People I'd met. Truth was, I had nothing. I'd been out of Wichita once, to Tulsa for a conference. The only new person in my life worth talking about was Devon, the woman I'd been seeing the last few months. I didn't feel like talking to Kristen about her.

Maybe the night might've ended differently had I been able to keep conversation afloat.

I told her nothing much.

We worked on our meals for a few minutes after that.

"Your hair," I said, just to say something. "It looks good short."

"Thanks," she said. "Yours has gotten long."

"Trying to hide my receding hairline," I said.

"I can't believe you let me shave your head our first summer here," she said. "Remember that?"

I didn't.

I told her I did.

"I was tired of you bitching about how hot it was," she said, laughing. "Afterward, I told you you'd better never grow it out again. You swore you wouldn't." She squinted, pointed her fork at me and stabbed the air. Her cheeks were red. "You were never very good at listening."

"Come on," I said, trying to sound more playful than defensive. "That's not true."

While we ate, she provided examples. Too many things I'd forgotten about. Years ago, I'd apparently sent her a bouquet of flowers while she was in Ohio visiting her hospitalized father. She claimed she'd told me a hundred times before she was deathly allergic to ranunculus.

I chewed, stopped paying attention. I had a hard time swallowing.

Martina Litty

SHOULDER TO SHOULDER

II.

Two men in a car reading lists to each other. Two men on an empty
street, their hands in their pockets, walking in step with each other,
shoulder to shoulder. Two spotlights on the trapeze artist writhing
in spirals: two shadows where there's no glitter, no smile, no light
anywhere. Two shoulders. Two shoulder blades like twins. Twin
muscles rippling: twin hands alight on the rope like gravity
is a playground. Two Berlins. Two Berlins like shoulder blades.
Two Berlins like a movie set. Two Berlins superimposed. Two
Berlins shuddering and stuttering like a spinning phenakistoscope.
Two boys dead in the street, lying next to each other, shoulder
to shoulder. If an open field is the graveyard of a neighborhood,
let this armchair be a tombstone, a flower bed, a resting place.
Two men in an open field. One of them sits down.

I.

We're on a train, we're in a library, we're dissolving
into the skyline like sugar water. I still have lists.
I still have to tell you about the newspaper caught
in the street grate: a broken clock, a white flag,
adrift and arrested mid-flight. Here we are,
nose to nose, as I could inhale you. If I could breathe,
I would inhale you. Here's the wall where you're
about to leave me. Here are your new footprints
like craters in a blitzed neighborhood. Before
this poem ends, you'll have left me. You've left me.
You step into time like a new pair of shoes.

previously pub. in *The Wall Where You Leave Me, INCH Books*

Andrew Bertaina
OUT WEST

I was living out west the first time I fell in love, tending horses at a ranch in Colorado and writing luxuriant letters home to my best friend. Mornings, I'd wake when the sun was a pencil of light on the horizon and rub the horses down in the gloaming. The air was crisp, clean and hawks careered through acres of sky. That summer, I pictured myself spending my life mending fences and riding alongside cattle, an image drawn from movies I'd seen late at night.

I remember—for what we remember is the strangest thing about us— steam rising from the flanks of a colt, and the black splotches that ran through its white fur, oblongs, rhomboids, shapes I'd see later in modernist paintings in New York. I remember its eyes rolling until they were a field of white and the way its hooves cut the air to ribbons. Up until that point, I'd never seen anything so scared in my life. Save once, when I'd seen myself in the mirror as a child, hearing my father's footsteps coming up the stairs. My father, from whom I was running like a bullet, I see now.

In the evenings, when the cold light of day had faded, turning everything—rock face, trees, meadows, horses—blue, I'd walk to a small creek on the property, a burbling thing one of the Romantic poets would have memorialized in verse, the way butterflies swept from branch to water, and the fish gathered beneath knuckles of roots.

During the day the owner of the ranch would stalk past the wooden fence corrals where I worked, looking at me from beneath the brim of his hat, windburned skin, eyes like flint. It was the sort of thing in life, which was to happen time and again, when I'd realize I was shitty at something I'd believed I was good at. Later, this would be true of marriage, of fatherhood. Most lives are a short history of such failures and a long history of trying to obscure them. I wrote to my best friend.

Down by the water though, if you wait long enough if you just breathe until you become as much a part of the night as the stream, as the owl, as the branches in the trees, if you stay there, everything starts to wash away, until you feel immensely clean. It's like being a child, bathed by a caring mother, held close to her, warm.

By mid-July, I knew I was going to be let go, horses unbroken, cows lost, so I tried to gather all the time left to me at the water's edge. I watched a pair of house wrens zipping through tangles of branches, snatching at insects in the summer air, pausing to fill the silence with trills.

One afternoon, I watched them darting through the brush and alighting near a nest two bluebirds had made. The wrens, my blessed loving wrens, pushed the eggs out of the nest, where they cracked on the ground. Was I the wren or the bluebird?

***

I wrote to my best friend again, knowing I'd be leaving soon.

I'll be fired soon, and I suppose it's fine. Turns out, the wrens are murderers anyway, pushed eggs right out of the bluebirds' nest. But aren't we all complicit in something we wish we weren't? Any life, if lived well, will have its share of failures and heartaches. I don't know if I'm coming home though. Every time I think of my father, sitting in his chair, sipping whiskey quietly, my heart goes quiet, empty of something essential I'm finding out here, maybe love if it doesn't sound too quaint.

What does anyone know about love, save God, who has an eternity to ponder it and still wound up killing, if predestination is to be believed, his own son. Strangely, those house wrens too, in their own way, knew of love as did the bluebirds and butterflies and lilies of the field. But what we all knew of love was apportioned in fractions, in different languages or nuances, such that we couldn't communicate what we knew to one another like the people of Babylon or a couple in a failing marriage. I sat by the water, knowing only my allotted portion, tender and small.

***

Son, the rancher said, you're shit at this.

And though it hurt to say it, I replied, you're not wrong.

Two weeks, he said, then disappeared inside.

I took the train east through miles and miles of prairie, saw a lightning storm turn the sky first that of a dim bulb, then a pale green as though the world was coming to a glorious end. I was religious then and saw signs of Christ everywhere. The rain battered the sides of the train, turning a clean and bright day into pitch-black night. I kept asking myself, is this it, is this the sign?

When we'd passed through the storm, I saw a young woman, her head still bowed in prayer, murmuring. When she looked up, I did the strangest thing I'd ever done up to that point in my life, I asked her where she was going. All the way to New York, she said. For acting.

My father was thousands of miles from New York, so I decided to follow her there, through great swaths of forest and lakes reflecting the moon and endless stars, wherever the train was taking her, it was also taking me.

You? she asked me.

I don't remember what I said or how our conversation fell into an easy rhythm, swaying with the movement of the train. Where was I going? I'm not sure I'd ever know how to answer properly. What I remember were the massive white clouds overhead, the giant shadows they cast across the open prairie.

I fell in love with her on that train because I was young and reckless and leaving behind everything I knew for the promise of something new, a pattern I'd repeat over the course of my life. And before the tatters and heartache and ruination, the first movement always feels so good, like the sound of someone playing the piano in a distant room.

previously pub. at **Bodega Mag**

Ursula Villarreal-Moura

HANDS ON METALLIC PONDS

Her religion is the power of suggestion. In the newspaper,
she reads about the nanny who stabbed two children to death with
a butcher knife before slitting her own throat. It happened on
West 75th Street near Central Park, an area she knows rather well.

For weeks, she cannot stomach a knife without thinking
of the stabbings. Wide blades glint like metallic ponds.
Her kitchen fills with muted primal screams and virginal
sunlight. It shudders with footsteps. She avoids the pull,
orders take-out, and eats in a hallway armchair with clear
plastic utensils.

As a troubled teen, when her parents reminded her of
her dishwashing duties after dinner, she often envisioned
whacking off one of her hands at the wrist with a meat cleaver.
Retribution for forced labor. If she wielded it swiftly,
she doubted she'd break the shock barrier. Five twitching
fingers: a Halloween prop, or the salvage of her own digits?

In adulthood, knives continued to haunt her. She considers
therapy to tame these disturbing impulses, but she's careful
not to taint others with knife romance.

In metallic ponds, minnows convulse like nervous blood
cells. Beneath the surface, a Loch Ness lurks in search of
believers.

previously pub. in **Math for the Self-Crippling**

Matt Mastriocova
APOTHEOSIS

We are pretending to fall asleep. The light pollution sprays your room so much it's almost like our own giant hagstone. We are not touching. You ask "What's on your mind" and I say "no thoughts head empty" but I am lying. I am a squishy stinky liar, but you know this. I am thinking about the destiny of all things: I am thinking about crabs. Again. You are tired of hearing about the crabs. Their cowardly scuttle. Their claws bent and beckoning like Thanatos. When I reach my arms out your body becomes a shell I cannot pierce. I told you this, once, and you said to drop it about the fucking crabs already. I tried to explain: If God made any creature in its image, it must be the crab, and he must be impossibly vain to have so many different creatures return to him. At least five types of crustaceans have evolved crab-like bodies. You didn't believe me, but the fact bears repeating: Five groups of creatures that have considered the crab and rearranged their lives accordingly. I understand. I, too, would like my bones on the outside, would like to crack only for the sake of being devoured. I want us to burrow so deep into the baseboards of the earth we hear only the rhythms of others fulfilling the silly little tasks of their lives. And how wonderful would that be? Just you and I, living together in God's image. No thoughts, head empty, just crabs.

previously pub. at *havehashad*

Despy Boutris

MOONLESS PASTORAL

Tonight, an empty sky. Alone
on the porch, I listen to moths

launch themselves into the porch light.
Some nights, I walk the roads

alone, let rainfall christen me.
I suck down honeysuckle

& hope sweetness takes root.
Ivy along fences, sky that purples

at dawn, angel white of alyssum—
the scent of someone I like

or maybe love, inked flowers
blooming from her shoulder, sweat

of her neck. I sleep best in a bed
of daisies, in clover that leaves

my dresses stained green.
Nature trying its best to hold me,

scent of mildew,
sky above empty, expanding.

previously pub. at **West Trade Review**

Jonathan Cardew
SUPERNUMERARY

Remember we used to deposit our bodies at the Credit Union, parts of our bodies we didn't need any more, earlobes and finger nails and gall bladders, paraphernalia really, frilly bits and bobs, doubles of things, triples, like who needs two testicles for instance, and who needs not one but two eyebrows, really eyebrows are for decorative purposes, they punctuate the face, they can be used for suggestion, like when you used to raise your eyebrows all the time, just subtly, like what was all that about, but then we shaved those suckers off and placed the hair into bank slips and there was no more suggestiveness after that, and in any case you can suggest in other ways, like with your mouth and your lips and also you can just say things out loud, which you did, so we kept our vocal chords, you're a very good singer after all, we used to sing in the shower together after sex, songs I don't recall any more, wait no, I do remember, we used to sing "Them Bones, Them Bones, Them Dry Bones" on repeat, in harmony, which was ironic because we were in the wet of the shower, but bones do stay dry in the shower, don't they, presumably, as dry as they can with all that meat and blood swimming around in there, but we never did deposit any of our bones into the Credit Union, it seemed a little ridiculous to do so, even though I did express a desire once to remove the bones from my little finger, to just get in there with my X-Acto knife and to saw away at the ligaments and cartilage and whatever else connects bones, makes them what they are, makes us upright and good stewards of the planet and generally individuals who have made sound financial decisions, because, ultimately, that is what we wanted, fiscal security, we wanted to watch our deposits grow, four eyebrows becoming 796 eyebrows, two gall bladders becoming so bloated from wealth you'd mistake them for small hippopotamuses with no eyes, no ears, no squat tails to whip away the flies as the sun set on another blisteringly gorgeous day on the savanna.

previously pub. at **Passages North**

Sarah Freligh
SKINNY DIP

We do it on nights when the stars hang low and heavy, ripe fruit in a black bowl of sky, nights when we're so stoned we make bets about when the stars will fall on us. We're always stoned, so what? The guy from Detroit is always the first to take off his pants, the last to jump in. *Snakes,* he says. Or eels. He swims head-out like a dog, coughs water, a pot smoker's wet hack. Years from now the cops will find him in a car trunk, shot once through the head, the pound of cocaine he was carrying long gone. For years I'll mouth-to-mouth him back to life, I'll dream him awake. He floats face up forever in a stew of stars, a body at rest patiently waiting.

previously pub. at **New World Writing**

Michael Montlack

NO ROOM FOR DREAMS IN BARBIE'S DREAMHOUSE

There's nothing left to daydream about
when you have everything worth wanting.

Walk-in closets crammed with couture. Ken waxing
the Corvette again. She's tried every damn career.

Another selfie featuring her dainty rigid toes
against the backdrop of her turquoise pool?

For what?

She discovered long ago this new kind of hell:
the redundancy of too much of a good thing.

When every day is a Good Hair Day, every day
becomes just another forgettable good day.

She wonders if she is a beautiful monster.
Why she was created to live such a curse.
Considers ringing Raggedy Ann or Holly Hobbie,
hoping they could ungussy her up. A make-under.
Just to shatter the monotony of her glamour.
But they don't own phones! Simple country living…

Chatty Cathy is sure to have plenty of advice.
All platitudes on repeat. More hellish redundancy.

Dressy Bessy would only want to talk fashion.
And Betsy Wetsy… well, that'd just be messy.

Kewpie and Cabbage Patchers? Way too young.

Maybe this is a job for Mrs. Potato Head?
God, the carbs alone sound revolutionary.

previously pub. at *Limp Wrist*

Julia Koets

FIELD NOTES ON LOVING A GIRL IN SECRET

There's a danger in comparing her to things.
        Her prayer, a stall of horses. Her anger,
the beak of a bird. Her sleep, a sun-bleached fence.
        Her sadness, a yard pile of firewood.

A patch of pines is all I remember of a field.
        Quiet, she says. Her stick-shift sedan,
her trouble with mathematics, her car radio
        turned-up all the way. I write her questions

on a sheet of paper so no one can hear.
        Late at night in my blue car, we drive
back roads, the only place we speak openly.
        The field's full enough tonight, I think,
to break into a thousand wings.

previously pub. at **PINE and Verse Daily**

Ben Kline

ABECEDARIAN IN WHICH WE
WERE SUPPOSED TO

acquiesce to condoms, to monogamy, keep
        our fists at home
        and online–our pride

buried by layers of latex discourse,
        rubbery attitudes never

connecting truth to the act—
        but where I put my tongue

didn't stop my dick—
        why else display it fully

erect in my profile's public album

focused on the pleasures my body yet provides–
        under *About Me*,
        the juicy details—

glory holes and loblolly ramble, a weekly circle jerk
        popular with the neighborhood

husbands, a few regular truck drivers,
        the visiting poet and occasional priest. Friends

insisted I get on PrEP when it debuted
        in those gleaming gay rag ads,
        but I couldn't

justify the cost
        once my insurance declined. HIV can't

kill you like it used to, they texted

with weeping emoji–*and we love you too much*—
as if I didn't

love myself enough to

mitigate my occasional thrill
     against a risk

none of us believed
     the pills relieved—we might not die,

only forget to take them, maybe suffer
     side effects, more stigma, letters
     from Grandma

promising salvation if we repent,
     if we marry, which we might soon

queer too, groom and groomed,
     dancing in fancy suits at our disco

reception, asking the DJ
     about a three-way after. Maybe

some witty man would
     convince me
     I didn't need to change,
     just adapt. Maybe

they would induct me into their home
     or their triad,
     maybe a polycule

usurping the mad notion I might be happy
     on my own,

vexing friends and the priest. The nearest bathhouse
     was a two-hour drive—

would the pills take effect by the time I strutted
        out of coat check to the pool? If not
        I could use some extra time to

x the smooth spot
        behind my balls, pack
        more lube and towels, hoping

youth springs from the tugged root

zealous hands were supposed to
        dig until I moaned.

Renuka Raghvan

DOPPELGÄNGER

Days after you were cremated, I sat quiet, looking out of the window at the fly trapped between the glass pane and the screen, buzzing and whirring, sending out miniscule signals for aide, the way its green, iridescent wings ombre'd into metallic purple, leading up to its giant compound eyes, a sight so keen, it got him trapped between two worlds—I could open the window and let him fly into the house, or punch a hole in the screen and let him fly into the yard, to freedom, but the next day as the fly's body lay there upturned and defeated, and all I could see was you.

previously pub. at *Blink Ink*

KOSS

THE FALL OF TOBY AND LADY

Before the neighbors leashed and fixed their dogs, they roamed freely through our fields, and Toby, my dog, courted Lady, the Airedale next door, who had nappy hair and bivits dangling from her shaggy ass, and who was anything but.

Goats climbed on tractors and ate my laces and jean-hems as they gazed with disinterest into my tanned kid face through widely spaced eyes. They destroyed things because, like men, the world belonged to them. And like men, people loved them anyway.

The apples, unsprayed, were for eating. Of course it was the Rogers's tree, but there was this sharing we did in the country. I ate them, one after another, tart as they were, 'til my stomach cinched, and I was sure I'd die right there in the crotch of the tree.

Toby eviscerated one of their white chickens in our yard, and I froze, legs locked in the shock of feathers. And when the chicken's life seeped out through her belly, and the stillness came over us, we both did a close-up inspection. Toby and I, heads bent and unmoving, made separate sense of his "work." Through his hunting and chasing, he always returned to himself, and no girl could understand or underestimate a dog's killing joy. I couldn't eat tomatoes for five years after, as they always appeared in my mind matted with white plumage. No one complained. It was the country and shit like that happened.

Up the road a body was found in the creek. Some said a man, some a woman. Dumped, they believed. Never identified. Next year Mr. Ritter shot himself in the woods. They called it an accident. All around, men shot themselves one by one. No one said much about it. Minding our business was best, Grams said.

There was Ben's bedroom gun-cleaning accident in the farm up the road. We'd see his mother, Pam, shift along in the store, her large brown eyes sunk in her head, while her pale twitchy hands wrung for decades… A few details leaked through the town. His bedroom was bone-white like chickens.

Toby was howling and I ran across the street to save him. Shorter than Lady, they somehow managed a death tangle. I ran back to my grandmother and cried, "Grandma! Grandma! Lady's got Toby's foot caught up her butt and she's hurting him." She laughed and I wondered how she could be so callous. It's clear there's always been something wrong with me.

In school, I could never summarize stories the way I was supposed to. My interpretations were always askew. And Mrs. De Vito purple-shamed me in front of the second-grade class because I never used purple right when coloring. She flashed my violet-striped boy, whose precise crayon strokes never crossed a line, and said "Someone is too in love with purple… Class, this is an example of what not to do…" And it was. To this day, purple makes me uneasy.

My third-grade teacher, Ms. Fuchs, was not much better. Spent first semester trying to bed Mr. Lovejoy, the principal, who was not leaning her way. Later, we found out he was gay.

She was totally different when a principal was around, almost someone you could like, similar to a limp tomato plant after watering—springing back to life—also likable. Gays must be the salve for foul hearts, I remember thinking. They fix all the broken things. The next year Ms. Fuchs bagged her a married principal, a short, large-headed man named Appleman. His son, a peer at my school, hid his balloon-like head behind a book for the rest of the year.

I still occasionally imagine chicken guts when I slice tomatoes and recall the yellow-orange macaroni I forced down that day Toby killed the chicken.

For a long time before I knew I was queer, I thought gay meant handsome and pock-marked like Mr. Lovejoy, with thick-legged German teachers who might try to fuck you. I couldn't imagine anyone sexing Ms. Fuchs, not because of her blocky torso, or her shapeless slack jaw, or anything to do with her looks—she was just slug-like in spirit, loved little boys too much, and mean as a snapper. But I'll be honest now; she probably looked all those ways because beings become who they are, like the devil-horned goats prancing on cars, not giving a shit.

previously pub. at **Bending Genres**

Richard Mirabella
THE BOOK I FOUND IN THE 1$ BIN

I liked the cover because there was a sexy man on it and I'm easy to manipulate, so I brought it to the register and paid a dollar. In the sun, I opened the book and found an inscription: *To Russel, with Love. John.* On the back flap: the author photo. George Willet. He had a mustache, the kind I like. I could love him, have sex with him, kiss him, be his friend. But he died of AIDS at forty-two, right after the book was published in 1987. I read the book, and it was about a young man in NYC trying to love other men. Failing. Trying again. I put the book next to my bed and thought about Russel, who this book belonged to. He grew up on Long Island, and his boyfriend gave him the book. John was an avid reader. Together, they read aloud from the book until they wanted to concentrate on each other instead. Fuzzy torsos (still in style at the time) pressed together, legs twisted around each other. John took care of Russel until he died, then John died. John's sister, while going through his things, found the book and it embarrassed her, but she couldn't throw it away. She too loved books. She brought it to a used bookstore. 1993. This was my brother's, she wanted to say but didn't, and handed it over to the clerk. All those years, no one bought it. Please, hold onto it for me after I'm gone.

previously pub. at **Split Lip**

Dani Putnam

TRACK: DEAD OF NIGHT BY ORVILLE PECK (2019)

Sparkle cowboy, flower rider,
horseback lover—
     shoot me saloon-style
in Virginia City, roll my corpse
        down Geiger Grade.
Just kiss me first,
   say *Country ain't your grandad's West.*
Tongue my hollow, I want to feel spikes
   rip my palate: *Country is fag land.*
     You're the daddy I've dreamt of,
the denim I love to press
    into my thighs. Your spur
licked my neck twice last week. I woke up
   dead each time.   The desert repeats,
see? Your fringe is the last sight
   I want to remember.   But let's leave us
     a mystery—
        ride to Carson City at midnight,
   I promise to haunt the pony
   tattooed on your bicep.

previously pub. at **Foglifter**

Kevin Sampsell
BLANK PAGES

Am I walking bowlegged? Am I pigeon-toed? Do my legs swing out when I walk faster? Are my shoes too loud? Does my body move like a normal body?

I told Peggy that I wanted a boyfriend now. That I thought it was time for me to try a totally new kind of relationship.

Do you want to have sex with a man, she asked me.

I just want to be affectionate with a man, I said. I want a companion to do things with and to watch sports with and to cuddle with while watching movies.

Peggy thought about this for a moment and then said, It's sounds like you just want a friend.

The man on the sidewalk asked, How is your day going? I noticed he had a clipboard; something he probably wanted me to sign. I told him my day was fine and I was headed to work. He just smiled, not even mentioning the clipboard. I felt like I'd been tricked.

Once, in a dream, my ex-wife tapped me on the shoulder while I was at a romantic dinner with someone. She pointed across the table from me and I realized I was actually dining with a well-dressed monkey.

Honestly, I must say that this wasn't a dream.

And also, there wasn't a monkey.

I don't think there was a dinner either.

It was just me, sitting somewhere, as my ex-wife tapped me on the shoulder, a candlelight flickering.

I raised a son but have never raised a plant. I have planted seeds and then forgotten them. I have walked away. Does this make me a bad human? I've owned more cars than plants in my lifetime. I am a sad destroyer.

Have you ever really thought about a key? How it's just one tiny thing? There are no parts. And yet, it's what separates us from the animals.

One word: hotel room

For a long time, I had a lover who called me "Mr. Bear."
I would sometimes call her "Little Bear" in return.
When we became *just friends*, I missed these names. I sometimes want to ask her, "Are we still Bears?"

There was a girl I went to high school with who was voted class president and was a popular, friendly cheerleader. I admired the fact that she went against the cliché of dating a popular jock and dated the cute artsy skateboarder instead.
A couple of years later, I heard she was working as a nanny for a family in a foreign country.
A couple of years after that, she was living in Seattle and singing for a band that was getting popular in the grunge scene. I'm friends with her on Facebook now and even though she hasn't been in that band for over two decades, I still think of her as being famous.

The simple minds tears for fears flesh for lulu Gene loves Jezebel Romeo void big country scritti politti the fixx haircut 100 ABC UB40 the psychedelic furs missing persons Shalimar sigue sigue sputnik big audio dynamite the wonder stuff orchestral manoeuvres in the dark

Edit: Instead of "her booty was doing something weird," make it "my booty was doing something weird."

The song that I have probably danced to the most in my lifetime is "You Spin Me Round" by Dead or Alive. The singer of that band is now dead.

I'm not sure if I imagined this but I think Madonna once said that she pees on her feet while taking a shower because it's good for her toenails. I have a strong urge to Google this right now but I won't. I'll just continue to pee on my feet in the shower.

It bothered me less to turn 51 than it did to turn 50. The number 51 feels sleeker, like it's standing up straight, getting ready to do something exciting and important. The number 50 seems too bloated and round, self-important and blustery. The number 49 is perhaps even worse. So clunky and awkward. I'd rather just stay asleep that whole year.

I look at the pigeon, but it will not look at me. I take a step closer and it flies away. It never looks back.

The letter L is silent inside the word walk.

At my funeral, I want the song "Endless Love" by Lionel Richie and Diana Ross to be played.
    There.
    I said it.

My last girlfriend would not shave her legs or her armpits or pluck the hairs from her nipples. I would stroke her knees and think of the man I sometimes thought about. We went to a sex shop and bought a strap-on for her to wear. I made sure it was a small one because I was scared. After much difficulty putting it on, she wore it with confidence, bouncing on her toes and making it bob up and down in front of me. I knelt down and took it in my mouth. I wanted to show her I could do it well. Any man, even if they think they're straight, knows quite well how to suck a cock. I wished she could somehow ejaculate on my chest. Okay, she said, and I turned over. I tried to relax, like I was getting a massage. She got our connection slick. She went further.

Sometimes a long walk will give me visions inside my head. TV show ideas, songs I've never heard before, new concepts for sandwiches, jokes to tell little kids. The farther I walk, the more of these crowd my brain. Here they come, I think. And by the time I'm home, it's all gone.

Kelli Russell Agodon
10 FACTS ABOUT LOVE

9. When one plans carefully, cholesterol levels
fall and divorce synchronizes with Swiss cheese.

3. Heart cocaine. Look into it!

5. When life becomes mundane, bring Valentines
to slide under the office doors of museum curators.

7.2 Misdiagnose *broken heart* as *extra dose of
the adrenaline butterflies.*

2. Sometimes a partner will find your death
is something they end up being complimented for
in regards to their coping skills.

8. You can also place Valentines on top of the refrigerator
we call Doom. When life gets dusty, they will be there.

4. Romance popcorn or stranger danger?! Depends
on the movie and person.

1.8 Nothing ever happens in order, sometimes
we throw the film strip on the floor
and start in the middle.

6. Your immune system isn't failing, there are people
in similar pain. Stress makes for flickering heartbeats.

10. It's chemistry when heartbeats coordinate
to wear similar outfits. Your favorite lover sometimes
does the same.

Nicole Yurcaba

THE 148 TH DAY

We stopped counting the days. I don't remember when, but we did. We stopped watching the news, stopped calling each other every couple hours to relay the most recent developments—the number of fighters trapped in a steel factory; whether or not Yuliya managed to contact her mother-in-law in Kyiv; how differently every reporter pronounces city names like *Lviv* & *Mariupol.* We tired of retired generals' speculations about a soon-to-be defunct army's strategies, its Soviet-era equipment stalled on a highway leading to a capital. We tired of people who know nothing about the way a thunderstorm rolls across a steppe where our grandmothers buried the German soldiers who'd raped our great-grandmothers calling us *Nazis.* We watched the documentaries attempting to read a madman's political diaries & wept at the scenes from Donbas circa 2014 because we knew an invasion's true date, & we knew at least one person in each village who'd lost a brother, a husband, a son, an uncle, a sister, a mother, a daughter in the east in 2014, 2015, 2016, 2017, 2018, & so on, & now we live our lives, waiting each day for a message from our cousins, our friends, our mothers, our aunts, our siblings about whether or not they're alive. Some of us stopped waiting. We stopped tweeting. We disappeared. Some of us went home & joined the Territorial Defense Forces. Some of us live each day with the anticipation of a grave. Some, like my father, stop in the grocery store after hearing one man tell another *Those Ukrainians, they're tough* & say *Yes, yes we are. You have no clue. Glory to my beloved Ukraine* & some, like my mother paint bottles using the careful brushstrokes of our ancestors & some, like me, bear our father's and grandfather's name & tread softly into the living room at 3 AM to stare at cousin Oleh's military patch, the one on which a raven sits tearing an eyeball from a skull, the words *Death to our enemies* stitched in black threads we can read even when there's no light.

Len Kuntz

S K I N

She wanted to be skin, to be empty, wise, satisfied and sanitized, purged. However, she took it too far and became bones instead.

Looking completely at home, she walked through graveyards where jealous ghosts coaxed her into reading them nighttime stories, news clippings with current events. Around the headstones the needy, greedy crowds elbowed each other for position, stabbing the air with their invisible limbs, one demanding a certain voice inflection, another a military cadence. It became so pathetic and demoralizing that the girl excused herself to pee and ditched the short-sheeted specters with their reckless lust for life.

Before dawn, she heard a garbage truck shudder and rumble. She saw it belch greasy black wigs of exhaust into the purple-bruised sky. The driver of the truck was a beady-eyed raccoon with foam in his beard and the other worker was a mangled possum, his head hanging loose by a jugular cord.

They smelled of whiskey and grilled cheese sandwiches, barrooms and insecticide.

She'd been taught not to take candy from strangers and not to hitchhike but here she was all the way across town and the pair of rodent men seemed dull enough. One called her "Soup Bones." The other called her "Skinny Minnie."

They tried to rape her anyway.

Now that she was a skeleton wrapped in a baggy of epidermis, the girl struggled to resist, but she discovered a can opener among the empty beers on the truck's floorboard, and she made mince meat, made hay, made a merry mess of her attackers.

The entire enterprise took two minutes.

After her pulse returned, she collected the bloody remains in a giant garbage bag. She built a fire right there on the side of the road. She cooked the coon first, then the possum. They tasted pungently exotic, like homemade deliverance.

She ate until she was full, her belly button taut as in yesteryears. Later she laid back and watched the sun come up, hand on stomach as if she was pregnant. She burped. She cleaned her teeth with a tooth pick and clicked her tongue, thinking: there's a difference between being skin and being alive, and now I know.

previously pub. at *Word Riot*

Aimee Parkison
HOUSE, HILL

In the hills behind the trees lives the girl I found by accident while venturing out with my butterfly net. Attempting to catch a magnificent butterfly, I captured her: dark hair dazzling like a midnight swallowtail sailing. She flickered in sunlit shadows like a wing shivering. Chasing the butterfly, we caught each other where I dreamed myself into a little girl again, my condemned house a cozy starter mansion full of golden light where cells regenerate, aging in reverse like memories. I forget why strangers say my house is haunted. If houses have stories that go untold, like lonely people, they molder in sleep, waking from endless dream. There is no such thing as a haunted house, our fathers say. Our mothers disagree and say how dare any man whisper there are no such thing as ghosts. The arrogance to claim what you can't see doesn't exist! Those who can't see us don't believe we are alive. Our fathers don't want to hear this, but certain people pretend we don't exist, that we're not real, not human, not like them. We are ghosts because they don't see us for reasons we can't understand.

Aaron Burch

THE LAST FEW YEARS...

I turned 40 and got a promotion and went to a lot of movies and watched
a lot of *The Bachelor* and *The Bachelorette* and the state where I live legal-
ized recreational marijuana then I turned 41 and went to the Kentucky
Derby with my wife and to Fort Lauderdale with my wife and then I
bought a new car and drove across the country by myself, east to west,
and spent the summer with my childhood best friends, then, at the end
of the summer, drove across the country by myself again, back the other
way, west to east, and then I got divorced and moved into an apartment,
taking with me mostly only the essentials and what was most obviously
mine instead of *ours* but also the big comfy couch that we had gotten
from our neighbors when they moved away and didn't want to take it
with them, and I didn't get internet because I wanted to spend all my
time just reading and writing, and I read a lot and drank a lot and listened to a lot of records and went on a bunch of dates and had a bunch of
sex and the city where I live opened its first dispensaries and then I turned
42 and then COVID shut down almost the whole entire world and so
I finally got internet in my apartment and started watching more TV
shows and movies at home and I read less and listened to fewer records
and drank even more—probably *too much*, but also very possibly the *just
right amount*, who can say, the world seemed to be ending—and then
the government sent everyone stimulus checks and so I used mine and
bought the biggest TV I could find that cost the amount of money the
government had given me and I started watching even more TV shows
and movies at home, but never another episode of *The Bachelor* or *The
Bachelorette*, and I went to my local dispensary's website and ordered
some edibles and then I drove down the road and parked in their parking lot and sent them a text that I was there and a guy brought me my
edibles via curbside service because people were no longer allowed in
most non-essential stores and some nights I'd eat one and relax into my
big comfy couch and watch a movie, and as someone who smoked pot
a handful of times over the years, here and there, but never really that
much, but who has enjoyed a large amount of art about drugs, I found
myself wanting to feel some version of my mind expanding to new real-
ities and to see new truths heretofore invisible to my sober eyes and to

feel and see and understand the beauties and possibilities of life—both *my* life but also just *life*, in general—and also the interconnectedness of everything and everyone, but mostly I would just end up falling asleep on that big comfy couch and then waking up in the middle of the night and turning off the TV and sometimes moving to my bed and other times just sleeping the rest of the night right there on that couch which, to be honest, sometimes actually feels like, if not exactly, at least a version of that sought-after mind-expanding new reality and previously invisible truth and beauty of the world around me, the very infinite possibilities of life that I'd been looking for.

previously pub. at **Complete Sentence**

Al Kratz
THE EITHER OR POEM

come on with the things that don't yet, yet somehow do.
we are all descendants of the survivors.
here's the problem:
it's not supposed to matter but it does, or it's supposed to matter but it
doesn't.
that's a hard way to hardly be living.
some brains are free.
some of the most ruthless dictatorships have been self-inflicted.
some are not.
never make a permanent decision based on a temporary emotion.
HA!
good luck.
what if God really had said good luck?
what if God was trying to tell us to get bent?
reimagine what reality has tried to erase.
people think "it is what it is" is simple, but then they do "it is what it
was."
steal all the erasers.
good luck, fuckers.
get bent, fuckers.
refuse to play the game of either or.
either you lose or you lose.
what if God was the original Gas Lighter?
what if God was a horrible Mansplainer?
what if God quit Twitter?
we are all descendants of the losers.
most people are horrible eyewitnesses.
we have either dodged the bullet or reloaded the chamber.
one time in tenth grade I understood parabolas.
we don't get to know either or.
you know we must waste some time, right?
one night a bug flew right in my ear, and I heard the world flying.
the supply and demand of things forgotten.
the economics of the fucked.

keep counting.
more photos of toddlers.
more photos of cats.
more hugs.
the economics of the space between us.
more poems.
more laughter.
the kind of laughing that goes on uncomfortably long.
the economics of either or.
the kind of laughter that feels like crying.
the economics of finding the comfort of dissatisfaction.
the kind of crying that feels like laughter.
I woke up this morning with a poem that's either brilliant or highly irritating.
some brains are free.

Larissa Shmailo

SPECTACLE IS THE FUNDAMENTAL INTEREST OF FASCIST ART

Come, hide with me from
their violence in the vi-
olets. They're soon gone.

Dawn Raffel

SHADOWPLAY

1. Visitation

I saw you again
last night.
You were smoking
a cigarette, which you never did in life. Your dog
seemed to know me.
Nobody spoke.
I wanted
to linger,
far from the firm, unyielding world of mattress, skin, walls, facts,
the knock
on the door that would not come,
the caw
of the living day.

2. Conversation

The women in this many-storied city have their tongues cut out. The lips
of the women make shapes, but no sound emerges, not even a moan. At a
certain time of day, when conditions are right, the women are enormous,
covering sidewalks, houses, municipal structures, blanketing the streets,
merging their aspects in seditious elision. They, among themselves, are
completely understood.

3. Gestation

Nascent in the swelling belly of the earth, beneath the skin of stone
and steel, beneath the living and the dead, beneath the steam and
the smoke, beneath the river of rock, beneath the shell of liquid
mineral, as hot as any sun or inferno, where no shade falls, lies a
ball of solid iron, under pressure too high for it ever to melt.

"Visitation" was previously pub. at **Exquisite Pandemic**; also "Shadowplay" is pub. in
Boundless as the Sky

Łukasz Drobnik
COAL AND GLITTER

We'll take this land and make it gay. All its plains and rivers. The Vistula will turn gay, the Warta will turn gay, the Oder will become gayest of all. It'll wiggle its gay waters to Madonna at her gayest.

We will come out to you time and time again. Make you look away in disgust. Pick at the many brims of your skirt with the multitude of your hands. Storm out, shattering the thousands of glazed doors. Give us a collective face slap. Hug us to your forever-sobbing chest and say you fear we'll be murdered in the streets. Some of us will.

We are the rainbow plague, the worst this land has suffered. Worse than town-slaughtering troops. Worse than child-raping priests. Worse than protester-strangling police. Worse even than neighbours setting a barn ablaze.

We'll sit you down and make you watch us in all our fabulousness. All the dykes and faggots and trannies of this land. Do a little lap dance if you behave. Feed you a Tatra-sized serving of glitter-stuffed pierogi.

We will celebrate queer masses, give out queer communion, wrap every Madonna's head in a rainbow halo.

We'll come for your children. Make your daughters and sons alike throw flowers at a year-round pride parade. Teach your toddlers to masturbate. Squash your infants into lube.

The death camps you wish to put back into service for us we'll repurpose as gay bars. Our army of drag queens will use the piles of clothes for their gowns, weave the hair into wigs. We'll karaoke our lungs away while prancing along the railway tracks. Put a disco ball in every gas chamber.

We'll take what never belonged to us. Shove the last of your coal up our fist-welcoming sphincters and crush it into diamonds. Make them rain down on the golden rye fields and smoke-spewing plants, the pine forests and landfills.

When there is nothing left but bedazzled wasteland, we will stop, the millions of us, and hold our hands in the open for the first time.

previously pub. at *havehashad*

Peter Laberge

USA TODAY SAYS THE PACIFIC COAST IS FALLING INTO THE OCEAN

But in the dream, it was new. It was
just us—just us down the curved tongue

of California, and the faux wind
of the Mustang you rented, it made

your quarantine hair a wildness
I didn't think to capture until after

it returned wherever it came from—
but the thought

lingered, even—hours later—in the motel bed
I dreamt for us, down the throat of evening, once

VACANCY announced itself, martini-green, across
our faces, even through

drawn curtains. The thought
lingered until the sun sputtered

back into the sky and we woke
to NO across the sheets, to morning

with bathrobes left braided
in a sleep-kicked pile, terry cloth still

slick with night, the condom perhaps
floating, bloated, in the toilet, another

slithering down the pipes. It was just us
     in that sand-white Mustang, and I spent

the whole day as I had all winter: thinking
     about every part of you I could remember—

it was then in the dream I realized
     what I needed to tell you wasn't something

I could tell you in a poem.
     It was something I had to show.

previously pub. at **Kenyon Review**

Nancy Stohlman
THE BUTTERFLY CHILDREN

I'd never heard of the butterfly children before I had one. Sometimes the angels descend with trumpets and announce the fruit of your womb and such. Sometimes it's far more subtle.

The baby arrived too early, a tiny larva so delicate you could hold her in your hand, skin like a September peach inside a glass chrysalis, half in the dream world, always. Thank you for saving me she said when she was old enough to speak. But she must have known what was coming: a pupa with so many legs eating to satiate a pain that would never subside. At the time I called it moody. At the time I called it a phase.

People think of a cocoon as something peaceful, a sweet little bag of silk, a quiet transformation behind closed doors. Maybe that's how it is for some, but the winds whipped to hurricane level, garbage cans flying around like cannons, and all I could do was take cover, grab my non-butterfly children and hide them behind a parked car to shield them. I tried to watch your transformation, I wanted to bear witness so you wouldn't have to be alone again, but I had to look away—your face ransacked, wings ripping through that delicate peach skin. If I told you spears of light stabbed the sky would you believe me? Don't look I yelled! For fuck's sake don't look!

Once when my child was little we traveled high into the mountains of Mexico to see the seventh generation of monarch butterflies complete their migration. Inside the forest temple, millions of wings fluttered open and closed in strange rhythm. Open. Close. Open. Close. Every trunk coated with a living, velvet bark, the forest floor thick with soft, dead bodies and tissue paper wings. In the silence, as the butterflies alighted on my child's nose and ears with their strange legs and eyelash kisses—I should have known then, shouldn't I?

And after the hurricane winds died down I found her wet, tired. Crying. Her delicate skin had become diaphanous wings like the most intricate stained glass, her eyes were spun sugar. I thought I would be beautiful, she said. Who will love me like this?

The butterfly children are born twice. Once to you, and once away from you. The butterfly children come to break our hearts, break them open. You cannot stop metamorphosis. You can only get out of the way.

The butterfly becomes a butterfly only after crisis, after a transformation both violent and profound. You are forced to watch your baby, dragged away. You do not get to say goodbye. What remains is beautiful and strange. The butterfly child finds its way into glorious adulthood, lands like good luck on the noses of babies and puppies. It never speaks of what happened before. But you know. You stop yourself from saying: you stole my baby! to this glorious creature. Because sometimes you can still see the larva's face in there, smiling, now always smiling.

previously pub. at **Matter Press**

David O'Connor
THE WEIGHT OF PACIFISM

The fissure between the doers and the talkers is apathy. The former wheels and deals in maximums. The latter leans towards fatalism. I tend to default to cautious, even precious optimism with a tendency to rent rather than own: socks, bicycle, home, supper. There is so much to do yet nothing to be done.

Even on good days, like today, a back wind glistening the sea blue, minor waves lap morning rain proved meteorology a fraud. At zero inbox yesterday, the doorman asked why I always arrive so bloody happy. I didn't say because I bellow through tunnels and plug delicious tunes to pump my diaphragm and lungs and throat into forced guffaws to jump start all dawn. I roll my Rs when I run. Write a haiku on the commode. Ignore all omens.

When the earth quakes, I double tie my laces. Can't sprint like I used to but can still truck for my age despite the accumulation of nasty habits. For example, I spend this morning vectoring the physics of story, wondering if what we tell ourselves is fact or fiction and if either matter. This inner tennis took a litre of coffee and a double ink refill. No idea where we're going but we're going anyway. When it takes twelve minutes to pack all you own and care about, don't worry I've timed it, to get out the front door and down the street when the tanks come rolling down the coastal road, then this illusion of lightness can turn delusional.

The trick is to avoid offspring, impulse buys, and carrying secrets. Yesterday my love said she would stay and fight. I said I wouldn't, not for money, nor nation, nor belief, especially something a subjective as freedom. Although I did confess to considering going to war for love. What value is survival without love? After work, I'm going to put a basket on my bicycle, one sturdy enough to deliver us all safely.

Nedjelko Spaich
DEEPER AND DEEPER

A city in the woods. Or a woods in the city. It is the lure of danger, the not-knowingness, the chance for an unromantic romance, a careless love, that draws us here into the unkempt walking paths of the park where no one walks, not a soul, except for us. *Hello*, I hear a voice speak into the hush. *Interested?* I wasn't. Deeper and deeper into the thicket I go. Some might say down the rabbit hole. I wouldn't. I could make myself perfectly fleeceable, an easy target, though I am in nonstop motion. Same with everybody else. If we don't find what we are looking for, we keep looking. A kind of hunt, a sort of search. Clearly nothing becomes us more in life than this specific quest. An hour spent plumbing the abysses of the grove, coming up empty-handed, I hear again, *hello*. It is someone else, someone new. New to me, anyway. The sun is setting now and everybody, myself included, looks just a touch more beautiful in the desperate, cre-puscular glow. He will kiss me, or kill me. Or he will walk past me as if he has not seen me at all. *Hello*, I reply. He asks me a question with his eyes. I answer with my hands. Seconds. Minutes. A lifetime. You know men—they come and they—

Go!

It is one of those false scares. When a distant siren causes all of us to scat-ter out of the overgrown bush like rats. He takes my hand in his and we run out of the forest to the edge of the river where we can be seen openly, as if we were mere passersby. A common couple getting our daily steps in before trudging onward home to make another complicated dinner and settle down in front of the television for the remainder of the endless night.

At the river, he laughs. I join him. *Close call*, he says. We are all exiles in the forest. Outside, we are adults. People with jobs, bank accounts, unpaid parking tickets. *Well, it was nice meeting you*, I say. He laughs again. An attractive laugh, an honest laugh, and I can see in his eyes a kindness that allows me, briefly, to get under the rock of who he is and why he is the way he is. *I wouldn't say we met exactly*, he says. I introduce myself. *But that's not your real name,* he asks. It wasn't. We laugh again. *I better go. Sorry we didn't get to finish,* he says. *You could come over,* I say. His hand leaves mine. *No thank you, that's not why we're here.* He walks away, picks up a light jog, turns back, waves, smiles, and runs out of view. Then it is only me, looking out at the empty concrete river, alone.

Alina Stefanescu

CELERY IN RELATION
TO NOT BEING VIVIAN

The man said the most important thing I could do depended on what the woman before me had not done. He removed the celery from his salad plate and laid it on the paper napkin where it sat, disgusted, faintly touched by an aura of sputum. He folded the napkin over the celery to cover it. *Who am I to you?* I thought without saying. The man said this houseboat was his, and the most important thing I could do was to wear Vivian's neon pink panties later. I didn't have to *be* Vivian—in fact, *I could not* be Vivian because she was curvy while I was a putrid stick. He said he meant that statement in a sex-positive way in that wearing Vivian's panties would allow me to be as sexy as Vivian even though I was not, and could not, be Vivian. He did not like girls who looked like they rode horses or walked alone in the woods without shoes. He did not like girls who resembled young boys from the back. He did not like androgyny, volubility, big trees, small breasts, or people who spoke French in their sleep. The man said the most important thing I could do was remember that he owned this houseboat, and he had named the boat after Vivian *before* he had acquired the pink panties. And really, he could tolerate anything—including the duplicitousness of certain pink hues— as long as I understood the important things, and saved those things in my mind like a list, and kept them in order as a woman would do for a man in a Leonard Cohen song. You are lucky I'm letting you play the part of a woman at all, the man said, seeing as how you remind me of a tree and a twig and a toothache and celery.

Kathy Fish

MOVING AN INSENSIBLE GIRL

\Moving an insensible girl.

She is cool and ready
as if she's been in bomb-raids
every day of her life. She
notices every
track & every sign. Once
she went to the butcher's, got
him to give her a sheep's foot,
opened it up with a penknife
to see
how every bone
& joint & sinew was made
& how it fit the machine.
She opened it up with a snap—short, sharp & sweet.

A woman who can do things
is looked up to—she makes herself out
to look like a hawk
or a dove.
She uses her voice freely—she imagines
a string tied to her scalp
drawing her up
to the ceiling or the sky
& all the rest of her
both inside & out.
She is a sparrow
flying through the hall.

* This poem is essentially a collage comprised of words and phrases from *Scouting for Girls: Official Handbook of the Girl Scouts*, 1925, Project Gutenberg. The illustrator's name is unavailable. The initial inspiration from Michelle Ross's collage taken from the same text, published in *Diagram*: http://thediagram.com/20_2/ross.html

Adrian Frandle

'LAST CHANCE'
SAFER MEN'S CROSSING

We hike past the final warning sign, then stop. With one hand I steady myself on the smooth trunk of a beech tree. With the other hand I shimmy shorts, then underwear, down past my knees. Careful to not lose balance, I unloop both garments from around blue sneakers. Watch how, naked now, save for my shoes and high wool socks, a red bandana knotted around my neck, we begin our winding trek toward the river. Dappled sunlight filters through the canopy. Puzzle pieces of light affix to your sweat-slicked thighs as you scale a mossy rock outcropping. This is no trespass; we will be open secrets now that we are in the shade. It is why we came. We have almost arrived at our destination, just around the next trail bend. Ahead is one last stream to ford…

cross cool swift waters
to be received by bare saints
who bear libations

Clementine Burnley
THE MISSION

From the white leatherette armchair through tall stands of wax flowers planted to screen the gravelled driveway; beyond that, the door and then, Petrolia. The sun softens the tiles, so that the air above the derricks appears to tremble. Sometimes, the wavering figure of a divine totters, then bellyflops between the laminated stems. There are no sidewalks, so doodlebugs and Jane dolls take turns with hostess trolleys. Divining rods probe the grouting. A Plain-folk Protestant is frozen on repeat, bright orange head nodding up and down. As soon as I turn my head the Petro-patriarch skitters away to hide near a tangle of buttress roots from the cars. In the distance I can hear singing from the distant lots where the geysers are stored.

Mike Nagle
AIR QUALITY INDEX

Sunday morning my phone warns me that the air quality in Carrollton is low. I step outside and take a few deep breaths. I can see what my phone means. Not great. Most things leave something to be desired. Let me put it this way. *There seems to be some room for improvement.* Recently J showed me a graph and the line was going straight down.

"Well," I say. "I can't say I'm surprised."

"Actually," she says. "In this case, down is a good thing."

Lately I've been drinking this low ABV cider from the Stella Artois beer company. It's called *Cidre.* That's French for cider. 4.5% ABV. Basically apple juice.

I can drink four or five of them before I start to feel a buzz. Then I can drink another four or five before I start to feel kind of sick. Then I can drink another three or four before I've made a huge mistake. Then maybe another one or two after that. Then maybe just one more.

Life, I think, is all about finding your limits.

Or, I don't know, maybe it's about something else. I'm usually wrong about what things are about. When I first read *Animal Farm* I thought it was about an animal farm. I thought *Gone with the Wind* was going to be a weather movie, like *Twister.*

To be safe, J and I and the animals spend Sunday inside. We breathe the inside air. It's triple filtered. Passed through brick, dry wall, and that pink insulation stuff that looks like cotton candy.

Funny story. My grandpa used to work in a cotton candy factory. I mean an insulation factory. They say that breathing in that pink crap all day is probably what killed him. One of the things. *A contributing factor.*

Outside, the air looks OK to me. It looks like air.

"It's more of an invisible threat," J says.

She shows me a graph and the line is going straight down.

"Oh good," I say.

"Actually," she says. "In this case, down is bad again."

Sometimes when I can't sleep I watch these YouTube videos of this guy who picks bike locks. The videos are like twelve seconds long. That's how long it takes to pick a bike lock. Bike safety is mostly an illusion.

Other types of safety too.

At night, when the wind blows, I can hear air getting into the duplex. Between the dried-out window seals. Underneath the doors. I've read that the air inside our homes is two to one hundred times more polluted than the air outside. And the air outside wasn't great to begin with. There's no such thing as a breath of fresh air. I think you have to go to Antarctica for something like that.

Last night while the wind was blowing and the air was getting in I was in the bathroom throwing up apple cider into the sink. I prefer throwing up into sinks. I don't know why so many people throw up into toilets.

"Better out than in I always say," my grandpa always used to say, the one who died of cotton candy poisoning at age seventy (at his funeral my brothers and I were shocked to learn that he had "died young"). He really did used to say that too. But even all these years later, twenty-something years later now or whatever it is, I can't for the life of me figure out what that's supposed to mean.

previously pub. at **X-Ray Lit**

Jayne Martin
PECKING ORDER

Our food, untouched and cold, sat forbidden until he had finished his. Tears only brought his fist slamming against the table, upending our dishes, twisting our stomachs into painful knots. Mother cowered at the stove, a fresh shade of purple blooming around her eye.

As we grew, feathers started sprouting from his pores. The larger we got, the faster they appeared until no matter how furiously he plucked at them, he could no longer hide who we was. His crowing begat our laughter. When he'd grown fat and slow, we cut off his head and roasted him for Sunday supper.

previously pub. at **100 Word Story**

Patricia Q. Bidar
WINNIPEG

They were 20 minutes early. Shan's boyfriend Gilles and his parents, in from frigid Winnipeg. Devout Catholics, they didn't yet know that Shan lived with their son. Her clothes were stuffed into the hall closet. She'd made Gilles swear he'd tell them on the way over.

Shan was still vacuuming, dressed in leggings and an old baby-doll shirt that read, Itty Bitty Titty Committee. She jabbed at her phone, launched a Stevie Wonder playlist.

Gilles was jumping the gun, having her meet his parents. But they were in town for the holidays. A drink and some cookies, which they would pick up at Lucca enroute from the hotel. The door opened and there they were.

All three wore matching red sweaters. The father was thick. Fit. The mother was pleasant looking. Like a wry school nurse. Hair spiky at the crown, with long, sideswept bangs.

"You must be Shan," the father said, coming in for a hug.

"Ha ha! I must be," Shan returned. Her head was clasped momentarily to the barrel chest. Gilles was nothing like the guys she grew up with in Staten Island. But the father? He was familiar. Not in a bad way.

Gilles held a pink box tied with string. Was the guy who'd eagerly gone down on her that morning in there under that red sweater and… khaki cargo pants?

The parents were taking her in. "Itty Bitty… whoa there!" Gilles said.

Shan crossed her arms. "I was vacuuming. Sit! Sit down!"

"I brought a little gift," the mother said. She held an African violet, velvety in its small pot.

"Christ. I'll definitely kill it!" Shan said. Didn't people water those things with eyedroppers? The mother looked crushed.

"Heavens, Shan," Gilles said, forcing a laugh.

Her good bra, Shan saw, was slung over the chair back. She edged over to it, but the mother was already lowering herself into the seat.

"Cute! A cocktail cart!" the mom exclaimed, twisting an earring. Shan recognized a certain eagerness.

"I'll grab some ice," Shan said. She'd picked up orange juice at the corner store. Hopefully, they liked screwdrivers.

"I'll help," the dad said. He followed Shan into the tiny kitchen. He opened a cupboard, found a plate for the cookies. Smooth in his movements. He smelled manly, like steak and cigars. A nice cologne. Small gold crucifix. Like the fathers Shan had grown up with and had thought about as a teen when she touched herself at night.

"Give this a rinse?" the dad asked Shan. It was an expression Gilles sometimes used, saying he was giving something a rinse rather than washing it off.

For the first time, Shan met the older man's eyes. And there was Gilles. But with a wilder current running underneath. Gilles had told Shan about his father's successes in business. They thought they could cut him loose ten months before his pension kicked in. He'd told his 28-year-old supervisor what was what, dicks in hand, at the executive washroom urinal.

Gilles had told his parents about his "emotional affair" with a neighbor. How he had betrayed her, Shan. It was why he was so attentive—to the point of irritation—to her now. It had been quite a year.

Shan took the plate. Soaped and rinsed, dried, and returned. The dad took a folding knife from his pocket and cut the pink box's string. He began arranging the cookies on the plate. Biscotti, butter cookies with jam and sprinkles, almond circles with pine nuts, nut meringues, sesame biscuits. Shan had grown up with these cookies, too.

"Here you are," he said. She turned, opening her mouth, thinking he was giving her a piece of broken cookie. Instead, he'd pulled Shan's bra from his trouser pocket. She had to laugh. She took the bra, folded it, and placed it atop the cutlery in the drawer. But it was Shan who looked away first.

In the living area, Gilles was moving the tiny Christmas tree to an end table near the front window. The african violet adorned the mantel. The tree smelled good. Sunlight streamed through and "Innervisions" sweetened the air. Gilles' mother used one hand to hang a yellow ornament to a bare branch.

"Ta da," Gilles said, taking the plate of cookies from his father.

"Ta da!" said Shan, inhaling the father's scent. He reminded her of Chazz Palminteri.

"Isn't this nice?" the mother said, turning. Both she and Gilles held glasses of wine. There was no reason to tell her the ornament was a Pikachu butt plug.

Shan slipped a hand on the father's lower back under his sweater. Gilles and his mother got busy refilling their glasses.

"Well, Merry Christmas to you, too," the dad said in a low voice. He covered Shan's free hand with his. A man's hand.

Shan smiled at Gilles. He smiled back. His mom lifted her glass.

Benjamin Niespodziany
MY SONS

FOR ZACHARY SCHOMBURG

I give birth in a hearse to a curse of ghost sons.
One won't let go of my hand. One won't nap in
his casket. One won't quote the oldest disease.
One won't bless me when I sneeze. One won't
stop talking. All won't stop asking about dad.
Their dad. "Where's dad?" They ask. "I am dad,"
I say, and my sons laugh. My ghost sons laugh.
We wear sunglasses. We dance. The parade
quiets as we pass.

previously pub. at *Obliterat*

Kaj Tanaka
PIANO LESSONS

Last night my friend Mary masturbated in the church sanctuary where all of us girls were supposed to be sleeping. I think I am the only one who heard the crinkle of her Barbie-brand sleeping bag and the squelch of her fingers, kneading between her legs. Later, after I thought she was finished, she started moaning loudly. I think everyone heard, but when I rolled over to her sleeping bag, she was asleep. I clutched my study Bible to my chest for the remainder of the night, her sexual dreams seeping around me like ooze. As I lay awake, I considered the possibility that there was some sort of other explanation for what I had heard. Her scream, for example, might have been a wild dream of bareback riding at her family's vacation home in the Black Hills; the wet rhythmic sound might have been the nighttime smacking of her juicy, perfectly moisturized lips. All things have answers. This is what God tells us.

Mary is my next-door neighbor. A boy named John who is older and has a girlfriend lives next-door to her, and after John is Ms. Radcliffe, who teaches some of us neighborhood kids how to play the piano and is known to be a lesbian. We all take piano lessons from her: Mary and John and I. John is the only boy in the entire neighborhood who takes lessons from her. Once I had a dream of standing naked in front of John, of taking off my clothes, item by item, and standing there naked and saying the words: *what do you think of me now, you boy?* It is wrong that I had this dream because John has a girlfriend. It is also wrong that Ms. Radcliffe is a lesbian, but I don't mind because I am not one of those Christians. But I think about it all of the time, John's fingers and Ms. Radcliffe's fingers and all of those other sensual fingers mashing and penetrating all of those vaginas all over our neighborhood. Fingers forming chords on that piano we all take lessons on—all of my sexually experienced neighbors confidently fingering chords on Ms. Radcliffe's grand piano—playing beautifully. And they turn to look at me while I sit off to the side, while I wait for my lesson. They smile at me, as if they know something about me, something juicy, something I have tried to conceal.

previously pub. at **The Toast**

Cheryl Pappas

25 QUESTIONS TO HELP DETERMINE IF MEN ARE BECOMING AN ENDANGERED SPECIES?

1. Why are men so afraid to be men?
2. What is the difference between being feminine and being a feminist?
3. What were the goals of feminism, how many of them have been achieved, and what has been its outcome for the beloved women of our planet?
4. What is the expanded version of the 10-second quote: "Hard times create strong men. Strong men create good times, Good times create weak men, and Weak men create hard times" as put into the context of historical cycles?
5. Who were some of strong men in history?
6. A popular buzz phrase these days is 'toxic masculinity.' Isn't advocating traditional masculinity bucking the trend?
7. From a temperament perspective, do you view President Trump as a strong or weak man and why?
8. What is Zeitgeist and does Trump embody it?
9. Who are the strong men in business? (Mark Zuckerberg? Elon Musk? Jeff Bezos?)
10. Man is defined by his work. Is that an oversimplification of who a man is?
11. Who is Stefan Aarnio? (besides a self-made multi-millionaire before 30 and 6 foot 4 inches tall and quite thin)
12. Why did you fast in the rain forest of Costa Rica and do you suggest others fast?
13. In seeking spiritual truth, what did you discover during your recent 40-day fast?
14. How can a man or a woman balance virtue and vice?
15. Historically, the term "Strong Man" has not always that compli- mentary, has it? Why do you use it?
16. Strength is often measured by muscle and machismo but is there more to manhood than this?

17. You like to quote Will Durant who said: "A nation is born a stoic and dies an epicurean." How does that apply to our modern culture and where does the United States stand in its historical cycle?

18. Back to philosophy, but not yours, this is a quote by Ayn Rand.. "A Creative man is motivated by the desire to achieve, not by the desire to beat others." Agree or disagree and what does this mean?

19. Zeitgeist: The defining spirit or mood of a particular period of history as shown by the ideas and beliefs of the time. What is the current defining spirit of this dot in space called earth?

20. You've told us a lot about what men want, but what do women want and need?

21. Is it possible to pursue manly goals, marry a woman, and have children, without abandoning the goals we have set out to do as men?

22. And let's say we hit it off with a woman and we want to tie the knot. What power shifts should we expect as we transition from single cave man into monogamous middleclass morality?

23. Chapter 30 of your book, "Hard Times Create Strong Men" is titled "Extinction: The obsolescence of man." What does this end look like?

24. In the book, you wrote: "The greatest generation, the World War II generation, was born in the 1920s. By the time they were 10 years old, they were living in the Great Depression, a hard time that created strong men. After the Depression, these strong men fought in Europe in the 1940s, storming the beaches of Normandy. Wounded or not, they returned home to build a house with their bare hands, have several children, raise a family, and work at a job they may or may not have loved for 40 years until retirement." Are we ever returning back to those days?

25. How can men reverse the trend in becoming an endangered species?

[Source article: "25 Questions to Help Determine if Men Are Becoming an Endangered Species," June 11, 2019, published online at sites.Duke.edu. The article has since been removed from the site.]

Garielle Lutz

MUST YOU?

I mention all this only because I was asked to meet the two sisters for lunch much later at a restaurant right down the street from me. They were both well into their forties. The father was long dead. One sat out in the car while I had lunch with the other, and then the first one went back to the car and the other one came in. I ordered a hamburger both times. Each of them ate a delicate miniature pizza.

Nobody had to put me up to this, and nobody has ever accused me of the things I was actually doing, just of collateral things. All the first sister told me was that what woke her the night she almost died (something had been coming up through the well of her throat) might have been nothing more than the sound of the fax machine cutting off a bookmark-sized slice of fax paper. It apparently did that for no reason sometimes.

I remember this sister as a stalky, underwrought thing, with surprising little springinesses to her features.

I told her I usually hung out at the library. I said the only books I ever checked out (you could keep them for three weeks) were the ones most loaded with bookmarks: discount-store receipts, business-reply-mail envelopes, shopping lists, coupons. I told her I asked nothing more of anything other than it be *replete.*

For a minute, there must have been a unifying misery to the two of us. It must have satisfied her, because she finished her pizza and went back to the car and let the other sister come in.

I'd better be plain about this other one. She had hair the color of cigars. She was wheyfaced, short-winded, whittled away by some sort of procedure. She said her husband was a man nowhere else in life other than in the marriage itself. The way she talked, I couldn't help picturing the marriage furniture rocking this way and that in the house all day and all night. Her speech kept coming out in sloppy suctorial evacuations.

What I mean is that it kept coming out and then somehow going right back in. There was very little net communication at all.

I knew where this was going. We were about to set off on the familiar path. Months later, hold after hold would have to be put on her feelings for me, but I'd still have the bloodshot regard of her dog.

I get sick of this shit!

I threw a couple of twenties on the table and got up and left.

The day was still young. I should be ashamed to bring up the man. He was just some man out taking a breather. I asked how soon the clocks would have to be set back. He said he'd have to go look it up. I followed him to his house and then inside to his kitchen, and he split open a bag of potato chips along the vertical seam on the back of the package and poured the chips into a big bright gala bowl. I'd never seen anybody do anything like that with just regular potato chips before. The sleek ceramic of the bowl was a glary madder-orange. I guess I just have a thing for people whose cravings are that placid. People like him aren't usually the ones to say, "You should probably go," after fingering something away from your face so gently like that, but this one did.

All I fucking ask of anyone is to be a little fucking feted every now and then!

I got my teaching job back anyway, because they were hard up. Nobody wanted to work. That was the first semester anybody in class ever took off a T-shirt, stuffed it into a backpack, withdrew another T-shirt, then pulled it on right there in front of everybody else. (His torso passed at least my muster.) And a young woman—this was during a quiz—took a swig of mouthwash from a travel-size bottle, gargled, then spat into the mouth of a Diet Pepsi bottle. (She'd studied, though.)

But why take sides?

Must you?

Let me just this once condense into somebody else's thoughts exactly.

Just this once let me be seated all alone at a big crescent of a table in a highway restaurant, a banquet place with obviously nothing on the calendar for the rest of the day.

People always wait to say "Fair enough?" until everything's finally in their favor.

Acknowledgements
from our Editor-in-Chief, Robert Vaughan

Thanks, Meg Tuite, for her skill and intuition, and hard work in assembling some terrific authors for Get Bent.

Thanks Joseph Young for his insightful editorial input.

Thanks to the entire *Bending Genres* team: David O'Connor, Samuel Fox, Meg Tuite, Chris Butler, Clementine Burnley, Jonathan Cardew, Keith Powell and Adam Robinson.

We want to thank every writer who has sent *Bending Genres* your work.

You make us who we are.

Made in the USA
Coppell, TX
22 February 2023

13197115R00055